Contents

Product Information

CafeCentra Client

Introduction

What is Earlyon CafeCentra?

Earlyon CafeCentra is a powerful billing and management tool for businesses operating Personal Computer rentals such as Internet Cafés. CafeCentra's client-server architecture ensures that billing is central and gives the administrator full control over his network.

The software allows account creation for prospective client users in advance on the server in bulk and the printing of tickets with account information for users. Accounts created on the server can be used on any computer running the client software on the local area network on which the server has been installed.

New Features in CafeCentra 4.0

- **User Account Scheme Configurations**
  CafeCentra 4.0 now includes user account scheme. This makes user account creation easy such that only number of users accounts is needed to create user accounts after user account schemes has been configured.
- **Limit Maximum Cumulative Time that can be allocated by each Administrator Daily**
  With CafeCentra 4.0, it is possible to set the maximum cumulative time that can be allocated daily by each administrator.
- **CafeCentra Server Extension**
  With CafeCentra 4.0 it is possible to view reports and create tickets from any system on your local area network. Not only this, policy options can be edited remotely.
- **Client Security Plug-in**
  Cafecentra 4.0 has a security plug-in that allows you to restrict users from visiting specified websites, prevent installation of websites, Prevent Installation of Unsafe ActiveX and Dangerous Programs, Prevent Changes to Desktop wall papers and many more.
- **Automated Hard Disk Maintenance Plug-in**
  CafeCentra 4.0 now includes disk maintenance plug-in that makes it possible for you to schedule maintenance to a convenient time. The disk maintenance plug-in will automatically delete junk files at a schedule time. It can also be configured to start disk cleanup when the disk free space falls below a certain level or even warn user when this happens.
- **Auto Deduct Printed Jobs**
  CafeCentra 4.0 now has the capability to automatically deduct out of user time for every page printed by the user as long as the user has enough time to cover the number of pages he or she needs to print.
- **Auto-Refilled User Accounts**
  With CafeCentra 4.0, it is possible to configure some accounts to be automatically refilled at a specified interval. This is useful for repeat customers.
- **Restricted User Accounts**
  CafeCentra now provides the facility for creation of user accounts that can only be valid within a specified time range. These types of accounts can also be configured to work on specified days of the week or specified computers only.
- **Client Computers Utilization Monitor**
  This facility makes it useful for café owners to know how their computers are being utilized. It also makes it possible for café owners to know the peak and redundant period and so make best use of the information for strategizing.

- **Database Auto Backup**
  CafeCentra 4.0 includes an auto backup utility that automatically backs up your database at a specified interval.
- **Remote Account Refill and Remote User Login**
  This makes it possible for you to refill Client accounts from the server and also remotely login user from the server

What is Spectacular about Earlyon CafeCentra?

While numerous internet billing software have flooded the market, CafeCentra stands out because of its unique features which gives the user value for his money. Some of these unique features will be highlighted below

I. **Advanced Reporting Facility:** This is by far the most powerful reporting tool any billing software can offer. This feature makes it possible for café owners to monitor every dime made in their Cafés. It batches the tickets into groups i.e. 100 units tickets, 200 units ticket etc and indicates for each group, the amount of tickets used, the amount of tickets unused, the amount of ticket created, the amount of tickets printed over a specified period of time. It also includes the amount of job printed by clients and the time allocated by administrators. Deleting client user accounts does not affect the income report. For further reference, you can check the topic: - _Reports._ You can also restrict the number of people that can view Report. For a further reference on this check the topic: - _Administrator and Administrator Rights._

II. **Automatic Report Mailing Facility**
With CafeCentra 4.0, Cybercafe owners no longer have to sit at their cafés to be able to monitor their operations. This new Automatic Report Mailing Facility can be configured to automatically send user's reports into his/her mail box daily or weekly or monthly, depending on user preference. User also has the ability to choose the report type E.g. Income report, Print Jobs Report and Administrator Time Allocation Report. For a further reference on this check the topic: - _Configuring Reports Mailer._

III. **Remote Client Task Management:** With Earlyon CafeCentra, the administrator can view all opened windows right from the server and can also close any of these windows. The need for this might arise in a situation where a client opens too many windows and the system hangs. You might need to close some of these tasks. This can be done on CafeCentra server. Further reference on this, check the topic:- _Executing Remote Action on Client Workstations_

IV. **Internet Connection Monitor:** CafeCentra can be configured to monitor internet connection and can automatically notify users when internet connection is slow. Users are given the option of pausing their timers on slow internet connection or continuing with the slow connection. If a user chooses to pause the timer, it will automatically be unpaused when internet connection improves. This is fair to both the café owner and the users. This discourages clients who pause their timers even when connection is normal because even when pause is enabled on the client, when a client pauses and internet connection is normal, it will automatically unpause the timer. Another interesting thing about this feature is that you can define the time out interval i.e. you can specify when CafeCentra should assume a slow connection. You can also specify the intervals at which CafeCentra would be checking internet connection. With this version, you can now monitor not only your gateway alone but your DNS server or any URL   On how to use this feature, check the topic:- _Monitoring Internet Connection_

V. **Client User Assistance**
CafeCentra 4.0 has made browsing easy for client users. With this version, user can now close all opened windows with just one single click. Users also can check the popular

mail sites like yahoo and hotmail with just a single click. Users can also add extra time to their ticket without having to log out.

VI. Improved client Security.

CafeCentra 4.0 is one of the most secured internet billing software. It incorporates a feature called App guard which is different from the client itself. This ensures that if at all cost the client is terminated it note the tickets and starts the timer again. If this happens again, it locks the ticket and notifies the server of an attempt to crack the timer. On a third attempt, it closes all the application running and shuts the workstation down.

VII. Print Job monitoring and Auto-Deduction of Print Cost: This Feature makes CafeCentra to stand out among all other billing software. With CafeCentra client installed on your systems, you can monitor every job printed on your systems. CafeCentra will catch every job printed and notify the user to either call the administrator to be able to print or click the print later button so as to notify the administrator after he finishes. The user can also cancel the print job if he did not print intentionally. On clicking print later button, the job is paused. When the user notifies the administrator, the administrator can either print directly from the client by applying password or he can view the print jobs on that particular client workstation, select the particular job and print right from the server. The jobs printed are then added to the incomes report. With CafeCentra, it is possible to monitor jobs printed from computers not running CafeCentra client. CafeCentra 4.0 now introduces auto-deduction from client user time for print billing. For further reference on monitoring print jobs, check the topics: - *Printer Jobs Monitoring*

VIII. Events Log: This is by far the most powerful reporting tool. It is not just about income alone but it reports every action on the network. With CafeCentra events log, the administrator can monitor and know every thing happening on his network ranging from printing of tickets, client workstation shutdown, creation of tickets, printing from either any client workstation or the server.. All these are logged in the events log. The dates and times these actions were performed are logged and the person responsible for these actions are also logged. With CafeCentra 4.0, events can be searched by date and also by administrator name. For further reference, check the topic:- *Viewing Events Log*

IX. Website Restriction and Junk Installation Restriction

With CafeCentra, the web site restriction works equally well on Windows 95,98, ME, 2000 and XP. To aid performance, you do not have to enter a vast array of sites to limit for example pornographic sites. A few key site parameters may only be entered for those who do not wish to include an exhaustive list that slows down performance. Even when users resort to using search engines to lookup restricted sites and try to navigate to view a cache of such site, CafeCentra totally restricts and foils such tactics, making its web restriction easily the most powerful available in any Cyber Café Billing and Management software on the market.

Server Installation and Administration

Installing CafeCentra Server.

Installing CafeCentra Server is a very simple task which can be completed within 2 minutes. Double click on the CafeCentra Server setup icon of the installation file *CCServer_Setup.exe*

A wizard guides you through the installation process. On Double clicking the setup icon, you will be prompted if you want to install Earlyon CafeCentra Server. Click Yes. This brings out the welcome to Earlyon CafeCentra screen.

Click next to move to the next stage

Click yes to move to the next stage if you accept the license agreement and if you do not, click on No.

Read through the License agreement and click on next to continue.

The additional task screen is shown next.

Check the Create a desktop icon if you want Earlyon CafeCentra icon to be created on your desktop and click the next button to bring the ready to install screen.

Click on the install if you are ready to install. A screen shows you the progress of installation. Choose the launch Earlyon CafeCentra and CafeCentra Help options to launch CafeCentra server and the help file after installation and click finish to complete the installation.

If you have already installed an older version of CafeCentra before, a migration wizard will be launched to make your existing database compatible with the new version.

Depending on your operating system, you might be required to reboot your system.

Starting and Configuring CafeCentra Server

After installation CafeCentra server is automatically launched else you can start CafeCentra server by double clicking on the icon which you can access on the desktop or by going to the programs menu.

The introductory page is shown. If your copy of CafeCentra was installed by an Earlyon reseller, you can insert the reseller code or just click on continue. The configuration form is shown.

Fill in your company information in the company information section. This is what appears on tickets printed. The system settings section determines the billing rate.

CafeCentra uses the concept of units to bill. You can now set the rate you want. If for example in the "amount to bill user per usage minute" box, you put 5, this implies that 5 units are equal to a minute. For more information on this topic, see: *Understanding Rates and Multi-Rate configuration*. Type the currency to be used. The "warn user when user time left in minutes" box is used to set the time at which the users are reminded of their remaining time. If for example you put 5 there, when a user is browsing and the time remaining for him is lesser than 5 minutes, the timer warns him that he has less than five minutes left.

After filling in the necessary information, click on ok. A screen containing the information you have entered as it should be sent when registering your copy of CafeCentra is shown to you. Click on close to continue.

The product information screen is shown. The information in first column is your Product ID. This is what is sent to Earlyon technologies to acquire your license key after you have evaluated the product and you are satisfied with it. For a further reference on this check the topic: - *Activating Product and Upgrading Product License.*

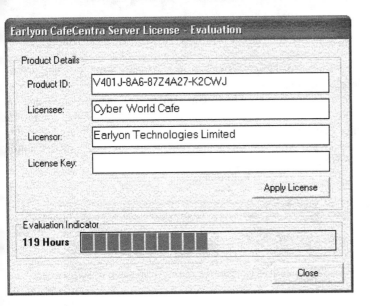

The evaluation indicator shows you the remaining time left for your evaluation period to expire. This screen is shown to you every time you start CafeCentra Server until you purchase your license. Click on the close button to continue evaluation.

The Login Screen is shown.

There are two default administrators that come with CafeCentra. They are guest and admin. The default usernames are **admin** and **guest** while the default password for admin is **admin**, the guest administrator's password is also **guest**. See <u>Understanding Administrator Accounts and Administrator Rights</u> for further reference on changing the default username and password. After you login, CafeCentra's main window is shown.

Getting around CafeCentra Server

CafeCentra Server is a friendly user interface with many of the often used features on the shortcut bar.

The sidebar gives you a quick way to change views. To switch to any window, click on any of the buttons on the sidebar or on the views menu.

On the menu bar are various menus on which you can access many commands on CafeCentra server. The shortcut bar gives you a quick access to many of the commonly used features like creating client user accounts, pausing all client user timers, changing standalone/ClientConfig password and so on. Placing your mouse over any of the button shows you a tip on the use of the button.

CafeCentra Server's main window is shown below

CafeCentra Server

To remove the sidebar, click on the "toggle shorts bar" button. The status bar below shows you the administrator logged on, a summary of clients in use and clients connected and the current time.

On the upper right corner, the internet connection status is shown if connection monitoring is enabled. The server's IP address is also shown.

Executing Remote Actions on Client Workstations

CafeCentra Server gives you the opportunity to perform many actions on client workstations remotely. I.e. directly from the server. You can select the workstations you want and execute any remote actions on them. To perform remote actions, switch to workstation view by clicking on workstation shortcut on the sidebar, select the target workstation(s) and right click on them as shown below.

To select more than a workstation, hold the control key and select the workstations.

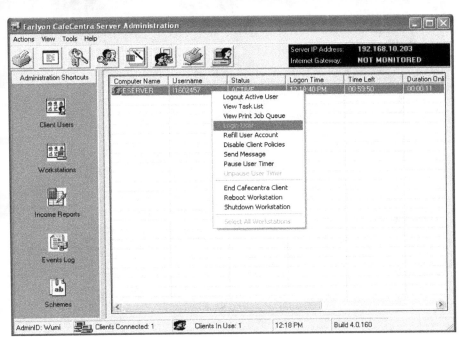

Remote Actions

The remote actions available on CafeCentra server are listed below:

- **Log out Active User(s):** Enables you to log out the selected active user(s)
- **View Print Jobs:** With CafeCentra server, it is possible to monitor print jobs on any workstation and print any job. To view print jobs, select the workstation and click on view print jobs as shown below. Right click on the job to perform any action on the job. **Note:** If there are no jobs on the selected workstation, the command is ignored.
- **Send Message:** Allows you to send message to selected workstation(s). To send message, select the target workstations and click send message. The message window is displayed. Type your message and send.
- **Pause User timer(s):** Allows you to pause timers on selected workstations.
- **Unpause Client User Timers(s):** Allows you to unpause paused user timers.
- **End CafeCentra Client:** Enables you to remove CafeCentra clients on the selected workstations
- **Reboot Workstation(s):** Reboots selected workstations.
- **Shutdown Workstation(s):** Allows you shutdown selected workstations.
- **Remote User Login:** Allows User to be logged on client computer remotely
- **Remote Account Refill:** This allows you to add more units to an account even while it is being used.
- **Disable Client Policies:** This allows you to temporarily disable some client computer polices until the user logs out.
- **Remote Client Window Management:** Allows you to view all opened windows and close any window on the selected workstation. To view opened windows on any client workstation, select the workstation and click on "view task list" as shown below. To end any task, select the window and click end task.

A sample screen is shown below.

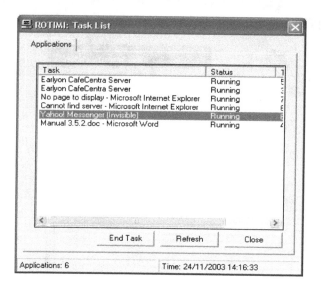

Remote Task Management

Internet Connection Monitoring

CafeCentra's internet connection monitoring feature is a unique tool for café administrators. It can monitor internet connection and automatically detect slow connection depending on the values you configure on it.

To use this feature, click on the tools menu and select internet connection monitor.

The internet connection monitor window is shown below.

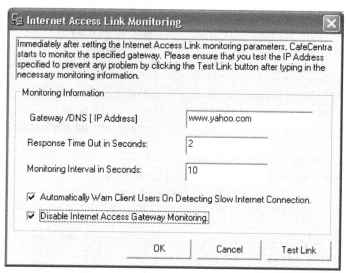

Internet connection monitor

Type the IP address of your internet access gateway. You can also monitor your DNS server or any website like www.yahoo.com. To monitor any website, just type the URL. You can define when CafeCentra should assume slow connection. In the response time out section, type in the value when CafeCentra should assume internet connection is slow. You can also specify the interval at which CafeCentra would be checking your internet connection. In the monitoring interval section, specify the value you desire.

Click on the test link button to check if the IP address or URL is valid. A message is shown if the address is correct. On the top right panel of CafeCentra server, the state of your internet connection is shown.

To automatically warn users if connection is slow, select the option and click OK if you are satisfied.

When connection is slow, CafeCentra automatically sends a message to all active clients that internet connection is slow as shown below.

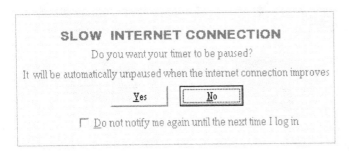

If the user chooses yes, the user timer is paused and it will automatically be unpaused when the internet connection improves as specified. If the user chooses no, then work is continued normally. If the user finds the warning a disturbance, he can choose the option "Do not notify me until the next time I login". The message will not be brought again until the next login.

Print Jobs Monitoring

CafeCentra incorporates a lot of options for monitoring of client print jobs which is explained below. To configure these options, click on action menu and choose server management, then click printer monitoring options. See Screen shot below

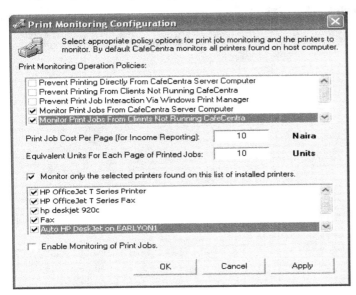

Select the options that you want and then click on apply.

Once print monitoring is enabled, whenever anybody prints to any of the printer selected the job is paused till an administrator authorizes the job. CafeCentra logs the Administrator name and also the number of pages that was printed. See Screen Shot below.

To authorize a print job, click on the print job shortcut on the shortcut bar. And the screen print job window is shown.

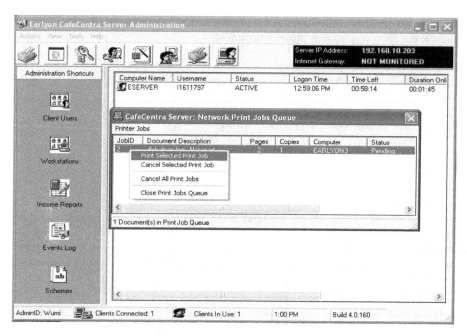

If the Auto-Deduct Print Bill cost from user account is enabled, the equivalent amount as pre-configured will be deducted from the user time as long as the remaining user time is sufficient to cover the number of pages printed.

If a job is printed from a system not running CafeCentra client, the job is paused if configured to monitor jobs from clients not running CafeCentra.

Client User Accounts

Client User Account Types
The 4 types of client user account available on CafeCentra are explained below.

- Pre-Paid Regular Client User Account
  This type of account is a normal type of client user account which can be used at any time as long as it has not expired. The user buys a ticket and can use at any time.
- Pre-Paid Time Bound Client User Account
  This type account is bound to a particular period of time. Outside this period, the account is not valid. This type of account is suitable for cafés that operate night browsing as well as any other special time dependent browsing. Starting time and hours from starting time are chosen. Once this account has been used before, it cannot be used at that same period of another day
- Pre-Paid Use Once Client User Account
  This type of account can only be used once after which it becomes invalid.
- Restricted Client User Accounts
  This is like a regular ticket that has been bounded to a period. It works only within the time frame specified during creation. Not only this, days of the week for which the account should be valid can also be specified. You can also specify the computers on which the ticket should be valid. To configure it for some particular systems, all that is needed is a prefix that precedes the names of those systems. E.g. you can name those systems **sys1, sys2, sys2** etc. To configure an account valid on this type of systems alone, just enter the value "**sys**" for computer name prefix. The accounts can be used at any day as long as it falls within the time range configured.
- Auto-Refilled User Accounts
  These are accounts that are configured to be automatically refilled at a specified interval. The intervals available are Daily, Weekly and Monthly. Prepaid Time bound Accounts and Prepaid Use Once accounts cannot be automatically refilled. All other account types can be configured to be automatically refilled.

Creating Client User Accounts
There are two ways to create user accounts on CafeCentra which are explained below.

Creating User without User Account Schemes
To create client users account, click on actions menu, choose client management and click user account creation or simply click on the create client user account shortcut on the shortcut bar.

Client user accounts Creation

There are two tabs on the create client accounts window. The bulk user account is selected by default. To create an individual account, click on the individual account tab.

To create bulk user accounts, type the prefix if desired else leave the space blank. The prefix will be attached to all accounts created for that batch.

Choose the expiry type. If you selected "expire after creation" option, tickets created expire the number of days set in the "expiry days" after creation. If for example you typed 7 in the "expiry days" box, the tickets expire 7 days after creation. On the other hand, if you selected expire after activation, the tickets expire 7days after their first time of usage.

In the amount space, type in the amount you want. This depends on the rate you chose during configuration. If for example you chose 5 units to a minute during configuration, to create 10 minutes tickets you will type 50 in the amount box.

To change your billing rate, click the action menu, select the server management menu and click on configuration. For further reference on rates, see *Understanding Rates and Multi-Rate configuration*

In the user type section, select the type of account to be created. If you have specified time-bound user account, the section for choosing Start and End time will be enabled. Choose the start time and end time. Note: Expiry type does not affect this type of account. Accounts expire automatically outside the period specified.

Specify the selling price and click on create and a message is shown to show that creation is successful. Click on ok. The accounts created are shown on the right column of the window. This can be repeated for several batches. To delete created accounts, click on the cancel button.

Creating User Account with Schemes

To create User accounts with schemes, click on the account creation with Schemes Button on the shortcut bar or go to actions menu, choose client management menu and click on Accounts Creation with Scheme.

The screen below is shown.

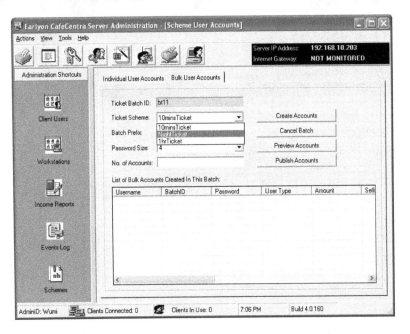

Select the scheme from which you want to create the user accounts and then type the batch prefix which could be omitted. Then enter the number of accounts you want to create and click on create accounts. Repeat the same procedure for individual accounts.

Printing Client User Tickets

After creation of user accounts, you can print directly by clicking on the print button but it is always preferable to publish before printing. Tickets are printed based on the format chosen. For further reference on this, see *Choosing Ticket Formats.*

To publish, click on the preview button and a window is loaded as shown below.

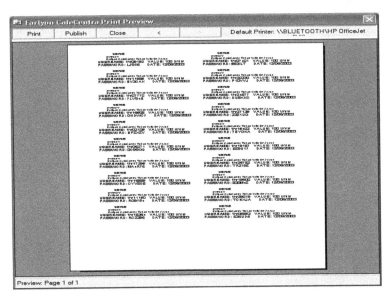

Click on publish button to publish to html format which would be automatically loaded by the default browser as shown below.

You can print from your default browser. Note: this would be replaced by next published tickets so in case you want a backup, you can save separately.

Viewing Client Users Accounts and Ticket Usage History

The "Client Users" window shows all active created client-user accounts. The sample screen is shown below.

To retrieve created accounts select the day and choose criteria if you w ant then click on the load account(s) button.

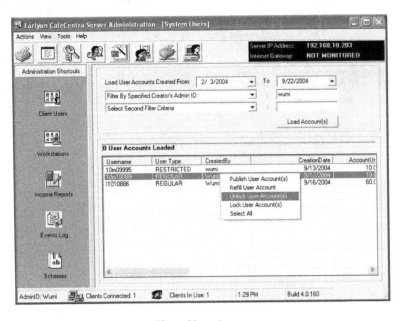

Client User Accounts

Accounts can be refilled, published or unlocked from here. To perform any of these actions, right click on account(s) and perform the action desired.

Ticket Usage History

Ticket history holds full information about a particular account or ticket. It shows if a client user account is still active or has expired. It also shows the last logon amount and the systems on which it was used. To view ticket history window, click on action menu, select client management and click user account history or simply click on the shortcut for client user history on the shortcut bar. See screen shot below.

Backing up Client User Accounts

If for one reason or the other, you need to keep your data, CafeCentra give opportunity to back your data up. To back up your data, click on the tools menu and select export user database. Select a location and type in the file name. Click the save button.

To import the data back, click on tools menu and select import user database. Locate and select the file and click open.

Creating and Configuring User Account Schemes

User account schemes allow you to automate user account creation. This implies that you can configure schemes for the different types of user accounts that you offer in your café. E.g. 10 units account, 20 units, 1hour etc. After configuring the scheme, during user accounts creation, what you just need to do is to select a pre-configured scheme name and the number of user accounts you want to create. This makes user account creation very easy.

To configure User account schemes, click on Schemes shortcut on the Shortcut Side bar or click on action menu, choose client management and click on user account schemes. See a sample screen shots below.

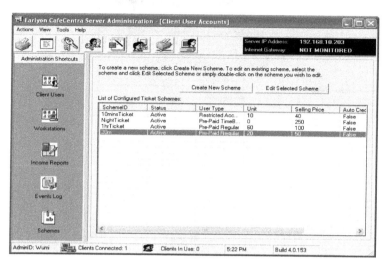

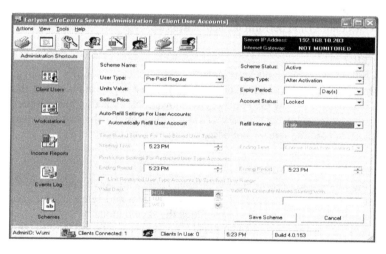

To create a new scheme, click on create new scheme button and screen above is shown. Choose the user account Type and the scheme name. The scheme status allows you to specify if a scheme is active or disable. A disabled scheme does not appear during creation of user accounts. This means it will not be usable until enabled. Select the account status. This determines if user accounts created from the scheme are active or locked. Locked user accounts are not usable until they are unlocked. . Select all other necessary options and the click on save scheme button. The scheme appears in the first screen shown above.

To edit a scheme, select the scheme and click on edit button or simply double click on the scheme.

Reports

Understanding Report Types

There are several report types available in CafeCentra, this reports will be explained below.

1. **Accounts Creation Summary.** This gives a summarized report on the number of tickets created over a time range. This report batches the tickets into groups e.g. all 10 minutes tickets are grouped together, all 20 minutes tickets are grouped together and so on. It shows you the used and unused tickets out of the ones created within that time interval.
2. **Income Report Summary.** This gives a summarized report on the number of tickets used over a specified range. It also batches it like the accounts creation summary. A sample screen is shown below.
3. **General Income Reports.** This gives a general report based on tickets used over a particular time interval specified by you. It does not batch the ticket into groups but it lists all the accounts used within a specified time interval.
4. **Accounts Creation Reports.** This gives a general report based on the number of tickets created over a particular time interval specified by you. This also will not batch the tickets into groups but lists all the tickets created within a specified range of time.
5. **Standalone Time Allocation Report.** This type of report shows the standalone and ClientConfig time allocated by administrator. It shows the workstation on which they were allocated and also the time they were allocated. For a reference on Standalone and ClientConfig, *See Standalone and ClientConfig Administrators*
6. **Printed Jobs Reported.** This shows the jobs printed over particular time interval. It shows the time the jobs were sent, the date they were printed, the computer on which they were printed and it also shows the administrator that authorized the printing of the jobs.
7. **Printed Jobs Summary.** This groups the jobs printed based on the administrators that authorized the job.
8. **Administrator Time Allocation Report.** This report type shows the time allocated by each administrator.
9. **Unlocked Tickets Report.** This shows the report of user accounts unlocked by administrators.
10. **Administrator Time Allocation Summary.** This summarizes all the time that has been allocated by all administrator during the specified period.

Viewing Reports

To view reports window, click on the "Income Reports" shortcut on the sidebar or click view menu and select income reports.

On the income reports window, there are three options to select. Click on report to choose the type of report that will be generated for you. Choose the time range and click on the view button.

A sample report is shown below.

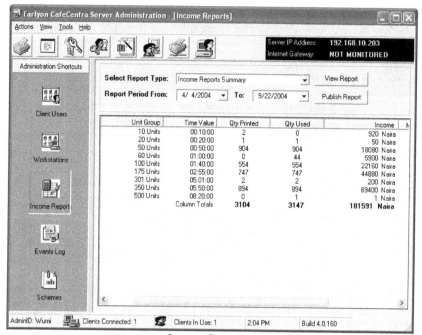

Earlyon CafeCentra Server Administration - [Income Reports]
Actions View Tools Help
Server IP Address: 192.168.10.203
Internet Gateway: NOT MONITORED
Administration Shortcuts
Client Users
Workstations
Income Reports
Events Log
Schemes
Select Report Type: Income Reports Summary
View Report
Report Period From: 4/ 4/2004 To: 9/22/2004
Publish Report
Unit Group | Time Value | Qty Printed | Qty Used | Income
10 Units | 00:10:00 | 2 | 0 | 920 Naira
20 Units | 00:20:00 | 1 | 1 | 50 Naira
50 Units | 00:50:00 | 904 | 904 | 18080 Naira
60 Units | 01:00:00 | 0 | 44 | 5900 Naira
100 Units | 01:40:00 | 554 | 554 | 22160 Naira
175 Units | 02:55:00 | 747 | 747 | 44880 Naira
301 Units | 05:01:00 | 2 | 2 | 200 Naira
350 Units | 05:50:00 | 894 | 894 | 89400 Naira
500 Units | 08:20:00 | 0 | 1 | 1 Naira
Column Totals | 3104 | 3147 | 181591 Naira
AdminID: Wumi
Clients Connected: 1
Clients In Use: 1
2:04 PM
Build 4.0.160
Income Report

Note: Any ticket used is logged irrespective of the purpose of usage. Also the income reports cannot be kept beyond 3 months before it is automatically deleted because of performance issues.

Viewing the Events Log

The Events log is a very powerful tool that gives you complete information about every single action done on any of your systems ranging from Server shutdown, client shutdown, client user accounts creation, client log on, administrator log on and so on. It also gives you information about the persons responsible for these actions and the time these actions were carried out.

To view events log, click on the "Events log" short cut on the side bar or click the view menu and select events log. A sample screen is shown below. Events are divided in to three categories. The events for the day are normally shown by default. To view any other, select it and click on the view button as shown below.

Events log

This is also a reporting tool but it is not about income alone. It reports every action on the computer including trying an invalid password or trying to do things that you were not authorized to do as shown on the sample screen above. Like the income report, events log cannot be deleted and it can only last for a month before it is automatically purged.

Administrators and Administrator Rights

Understanding Administrator Accounts and Administrator Rights

CafeCentra gives the opportunity to create different administrator accounts with different administrative rights and also has 2 default client administrators which cannot be created or changed. These two client administrators are "ClientConfig" and "Standalone". These will be explained later

Administrator Accounts. These types of administrator accounts can be created with different rights. This administrator type can be created as many times as possible. The rights available to this type of account can vary from one administrator to another.

This administrator account type can be used both on the Server and the client depending on the rights assigned to it. To create Café administrators, see *Creating Administrator Accounts and Administrator Rights.* The default administrator accounts that come with CafeCentra are **Admin** and **guest**. Admin has full rights both on the server and client. The default password is "**admin**". The guest password is also **guest** and does not have any right both on the client and on the server.

Creating Administrators Accounts and Rights

CafeCentra gives you the opportunity of creating administrators with different levels of rights. To create administrator with different rights, you first create rights and then assign administrators to any rights. For example, you might have different categories of staff and you might want them to have different rights on CafeCentra. Now what you first do is to create the different rights and start assigning administrator to those rights as you desire. For example you might want to create the managers rights and staff rights. You first create a manager RightsID e.g. senior staff, and then you start adding the rights you want to senior staff. Then you create staff rights by creating a RightsID for staff e.g. Staff1 and start adding rights to staff1. Then you can now start creating administrator and start assigning them to the rights you have already created. Now assuming you have 2 managers and you want them to be able to have the same level of access or rights, you attach both of them to senior staff. Also assuming you have 5 café operators and you want all of them to be on the same level, you attach them to staff1 during creation of administrators.

Now let's go through the process of creating administrator with rights. We will first create the rights for the administrator account we want to create.

To create Administrator Rights, click on Actions menu, select Server management and click on Administrator Accounts. The Administrators Access window is displayed as shown below.

Click on the Rights Tab, the default RightsIDs are **admin** which has full rights and **guest** which has no right. Click on the "New" button to create new rights group. The Access Rights section is enabled, type in the new rights ID e.g. "owner". The new rightsID has no rights at all. Choose the rights you want to be available to the new rightsID and click the Update button. You can create as many rightsID as you want and choose rights available to them. Whenever you edit any rightsID, click on the Update button to effect the changes. To edit any rights, select the rightsID in the existing and click edit. After editing, click on the update button.

To create administrators, click on the Administrators tab and click on the "New" button as shown below.

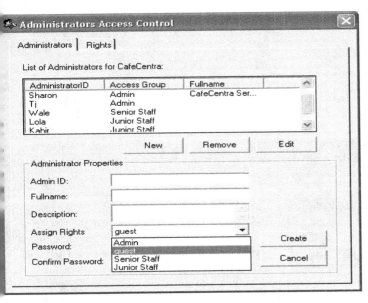

Administrators

Type the Admin ID. The full name and description are optional. In the Admin Group ID field, choose the access group which you want to assign the administrator to as shown above. This implies that the administrator will have all the rights available in the access group. Different administrator can be assigned to the same access group.

Type in the password and retype to confirm. Click on the Create button.

To make changes to created administrator, select the administrator and click the Edit button. The Create button caption would change to Update and click the Update button to apply the changes. To delete administrators, select the administrator and click on the Remove button. You can create as many administrators as you wish. To edit and Administrator, select the administrator and click on Edit button. After editing, click on update.

Administrator Wizard

Administrator wizard offers you a simple way of creating administrator accounts on CafeCentra server without having to create the access group.

To create administrator with wizard, click on Actions menu, choose server management and then click on Administrator wizard menu. See sample screen shot below

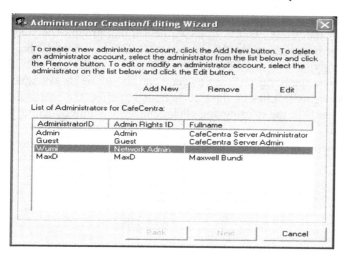

Click on the Add New button to create a new administrator or Edit button to edit an existing administrator. Enter the user name and password. Enter the full name and description if you deem it necessary and click next. A screen for choosing the right for the administrator is shown. After selecting the rights you would want the administrator to have, click on finish button. CafeCentra automatically creates a right group and names it as the admin ID.

Switching Administrator.

CafeCentra give you the opportunity to switch administrator easily without having to logout. To switch to another administrator account, click on actions menu then click switch administrator or simply press Ctrl + L. Type your admin username and password and click ok. To switch to guest administrator, you do not need to input your username and password. Just a single click enables you to switch to guest administrator. To switch to guest administrator, click on actions menu and then click switch to guest administrator or Press ctrl + G.

Changing Administrator Password

You can easily change your administrator password by clicking on Actions menu and then click on Server Management. Click on administrator password. Type in your username and your current password and then type your new password in the space provided. Type in your new password again to confirm and click on Ok button.

ClientConfig Administrator.

This administrator is valid only on the client. This account has full rights on the client and can allocate any amount of time. This account is useful in case the server has a problem and cannot be started. ClientConfig can shutdown or reboot the client computer. It can also disable the policies on client and can even remove the client software. The username is "ClientConfig" which cannot be changed and the default password is "password." To change the password, click on edit standalone property button on the shortcut bar and select ClientConfig. Change the password and click ok. To view ClientConfig password, choose the show administrator password in clear text option.

Standalone Administrator.

This administrator can only be used on the client. This type of administrator can only allocate time on the client. This is also useful in a case where by the server is not running. The maximum time that can be allocated by standalone administrator is configurable. Standalone can also be disabled if server is running. The Username which cannot be changed is "**standalone**" and password is "**password**". To change the password, click on the "Edit workstation property." button on the shortcut bar. Standalone is selected by default, edit the password as desired and click Ok. . To view standalone password, choose the show administrator password in clear text option.

The change is effected immediately on the client computers.

Policy Settings

Understanding Policy Settings

CafeCentra has a lot of policies that can help you to manage your café. CafeCentra Policies are categorised into three groups namely

System Policies

These policies are system specific i.e. they affect the operating system directly and are implemented on the client machine. To enable or disable some of these policies, you might be required to reboot your system. A sample screen is shown below.

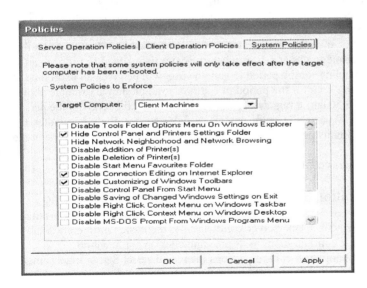

Client Operation Policies.

This category of policies deal with client operations. These policies affect CafeCentra client only. Examples of these types of policies are enabling or disabling pause on client timer, enabling of print jobs monitoring and so on.

Server Operation Policies

These are implemented only on CafeCentra server. They are policies like locking of system time, prevent client not running CafeCentra client from printing, prevent printing directly from server machine, load CafeCentra Server on windows start up etc.

Applying Policy Settings

To apply policies, click on the actions menu and select server management and click policy settings. On the policy setting windows, there are three tabs: - the Client Operation Policies tab, Server Operation Policies tab and the System Policies tab.

Select the policies you want and click the OK button. You are prompted to reboot your workstations. This is because some of the system policies would not take effect until you reboot your system. Click the Yes button to reboot immediately or click No to reboot manually whenever you wish.

Billing Rates and General Configuration.

Understanding Rates and Multi-Rate configuration

CafeCentra uses the concept of units to bill client users. Immediately after installation, if you configured CafeCentra to bill at the rate of 5 units per minute, it implies that each minute amounts to 5 units on CafeCentra. This means that creating a 50 unit account will amount to a 10 minutes ticket since 5 units is equal to a minute.

Multi-rate Configuration ensures that you can change the billing rate for different period of time without creating new accounts. Assuming you configure 5 units to a minute as earlier stated, it means that a user that buys a150 units ticket has 30 minutes. Now you might want to give extra time to people who come between a particular period of time. E.g. you want to give extra 20 minutes to people who come between 9am and 10 am. All you will just need to do is to configure CafeCentra to equate 3 units to a minute between 9am and 10am.This implies that anybody that comes to browse with a 150 units ticket between 9am and 10am i.e. has 50 minutes while at any other period outside this, the person has 30 minutes on that same ticket. Note if a person comes at a time when the extra time added to his account is greater than the time remaining for the period to end, the user will be given an extra time in proportion to the remaining time for the period to end. For example in the example above, if a person come around 9.50 am, it remains 10 minute for the period to end but the person should have 20 minutes. What CafeCentra does is to calculate the first 10 minutes the person has at the rate of 3 units per minutes and calculates the rest of the user's time at the default rate.

Note: Multi-rate billing does not affect Time-Bound User Accounts

Changing Configuration Settings and Enabling Multi-Rate Billing.

If you want to change the configurations you chose after installation, click on actions menu and select Server management. Click Server configuration, the basic configuration tab is chosen by default. Change configurations as desired and click on apply button.

To configure multi-rate billing, also click on actions menu and select Server management. Click Server configuration and choose multi-rate billing tab. Choose the periods and input the rates as desired. Choose the Enable multi-rate billing of browsing time and click on the apply button.

Configuring Ticket Format

CafeCentra give the opportunity to choose different ticket formats for printing of tickets. The 3 ticket formats available in CafeCentra are:

1. **Compact Format**. This contains minimum information and will contain 36 on an A4 paper
2. **Standard Format**: This contains average information ranging from creation date to expiry time. It contains 26 tickets on an A4 paper
3. **Informational Format**. This contains all information about the café and also gives space for additional information. It will contain 20 tickets on an A4 paper
4. **Elegant Format**. Shows the same information same as standard but with a different font. It will contain 20 tickets on an A4 paper with spaces in between each row.

To choose a ticket format, click on actions menu and click on server management. Click ticket formats.

Configuring Special Computer Rates

With CafeCentra, it is possible to bill different computer at different rates. This ensures that you do not have to create separate tickets for special computers. Assuming you have some special computers and you want to bill at a higher rate on those systems you can configure CafeCentra to bill at a rate higher than normal workstations. Since CafeCentra uses the concept of units to bill this is very easy. CafeCentra bills special computers in multiple of rates. For example if you have a default rate of 5 units to a minute, to configure workstations to bill at a higher rate you will configure CafeCentra to multiply the default rate by a value greater than one for that computer i.e. 2 such that for that computer, the billing rate will now be 10 units per minutes.

To Configure Special Computer billing, click on actions menu and click on Server Management. Click on Server Configuration and then click on the Special Computers tab Add workstation name and add the rate multiplier. Add as many workstations as desired and choose the Enable Special Computers option. Click on the Apply button.

Note: Multi-rate billing also affects special computers. I.e. The multiplier configured is used to multiply the active rate if a browser comes at period when multi-rate billing is active.

Configuring Reports Mailer

CafeCentra Makes it possible for you to know exactly what is going on in your café through it Report mailing capability.

You can configure CafeCentra to mail your report to you daily, weekly or monthly. CafeCentra send your report such that it is not fragmented. If you have chosen daily, it sends yesterday's report today and sends today's report tomorrow such that it is able to send a whole day's report without fragmentation. It does the same thing for weekly and monthly.

You can also choose the types of reports that CafeCentra would be sending to you. These report types are Income report, Printed Jobs report, Admin Time Allocation report, unlocked tickets report, system Utilization report.

To enable this feature, click on Actions menu and click on server management. Click on the Income report Mailer. Fill in the email address that CafeCentra should mail the reports to and choose the types of report s you want. Choose the sending interval and click Enable Mailing of CafeCentra Reports. Click on the Apply button

Note: The reports sent by CafeCentra might be considered as spam by some mailing system so it is always advisable for you to check your bulk or spam mail folder.

Product Information

Viewing Product Information

You can view your product information to see if you are using a licensed copy of CafeCentra or you are still evaluating it and the number of client user license you have bought by clicking on the help menu and clicking on Product License Information. The screen below is shown.

Using CafeCentra Online Help

CafeCentra offers a quick reference to users. To access the quick user reference that comes with CafeCentra, click on the help menu and select help contents.

To use the online help that comes with CafeCentra, click on the start menu, navigate to CafeCentra and click CafeCentra HTML help.

You can also visit the CafeCentra site for online support tips by selecting the help menu and clicking on CafeCentra online support tips.

Activating and Upgrading CafeCentra License

After exhausting the evaluation period for CafeCentra, if you desire to purchase a licensed copy of CafeCentra, copy the product ID shown on the license screen shown above and mail to info@cafecentra.com with the payment details. Your license key is generated and mailed to you. Copy and paste the license key and click on apply. A message is shown to notify you that your copy is licensed.

You can display the license screen by starting cafecentra. To upgrade CafeCentra, click on the help menu and select upgrade license on next run. The next time you start CafeCentra, the license screen is displayed.

CafeCentra Client

Installing CafeCentra client

To install CafeCentra client, double click the CafeCentra setup icon. A wizard guides you through the process of installation. After the installation process, you will need point CafeCentra Client to the machine on which CafeCentra server is running as shown below.

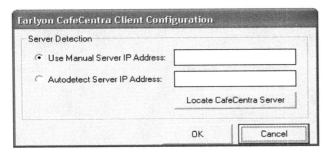

To manually locate CafeCentra Server, enter your Server IP address and click on the Locate CafeCentra Client button or choose the Autodetect Server IP Address option and click Locate Cafecentra Server to automatically detect CafeCentra Server.

Logging into CafeCentra Client as an Administrator.

You can log into CafeCentra client as either an administrator or as a regular user.

To log in as an administrator, click anywhere on cafecentra client. Type your username and password and click on the login as administrator then click Ok. For a further reference on this topic, check. *Understanding Administrator Accounts and Administrator Rights*

The Administrator window is displayed. You can allocate time on the Administrator panel or perform any administrative task depending on the rights assigned to you as shown below.

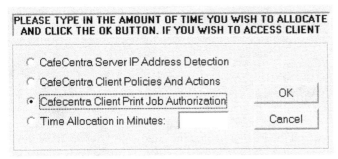

If you want to perform any other task other than allocating time, the panel shown below is brought to you. You can perform any action on the pane ranging from shutting down the workstation to disabling policies and so on.

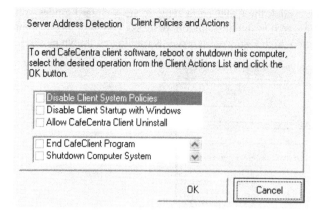

Client Administration

If you log into CafeCentra Client with tickets, a screen is shown to you to indicate the minutes you have on your ticket if the account is valid. A sample screen is shown below.

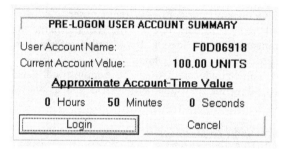

Click the Login button to login or click cancel.

Locating CafeCentra Server

To manually locate CafeCentra server if auto scan (DHCP) is not enabled, log into CafeCentra client as an administrator and click on the advance Button. Choose the Server IP option and enter your Server's IP address or choose the Auto detect Server IP address detection option. Click on the Locate CafeCentra Server button. A message is shown to indicate successful connection.

Click on Ok and CafeCentra client will connect to the server.

Using CafeCentra Client User Options.

Cafecentra offers some options to client users. These options are Pause Client User, View Pending Print Jobs, Combine User Accounts and Search the Web. Users can also close all opened windows with just a single click and also check popular mail sites like yahoo and hotmail with just a single click. To access any of these options, log into CafeCentra Client and click on the Option button.

These options can be disabled or enabled from the server as the administrator wishes.
A sample screen is shown below.

Earlyon CafeCentra Version 4.0 User Manual

The latest version of Earlyon CafeCentra is always available for download on the web at http://www.cafecentra.com
You can also access up to date user tips and information at www.cafecentra.com/tips.htm
To contact the Earlyon CafeCentra development team Call: 0803-4521607 Or
Email: info@cafecentra.com

www.ingramcontent.com/pod-product-compliance
Lightning Source LLC
Chambersburg PA
CBHW060937050326

40689CB00013B/3126